WOKING AS IT WAS

# WOKING
## AS IT WAS

## Iain Wakeford

## Phillimore

1985

Published by
PHILLIMORE & CO. LTD.
Shopwyke Hall, Chichester, Sussex

ISBN 0 85033 597 3

Printed and bound in Great Britain by
BIDDLES LIMITED
Guildford, Surrey

*To my niece, Kerry*

# LIST OF ILLUSTRATIONS

# ACKNOWLEDGEMENTS

Once again I would like to thank everyone who has lent me photographs for my project. Most of all I would like to thank the following for allowing me to use their old pictures and documents in this book, and for giving me information for the captions: Mrs. P. Andrews, Mr. R. Best, Mr. A. Boarer, Mrs. K. Bowerman, Mr. H. Boxall, Mr. N. Burnett, Mrs. M. Campbell, Mr. D. Chapman, Mrs. E. Cuttle, Mrs. Eales, Mr. S. Eaves, Mr. B. Elkins, Mrs. Fisher, Mrs. Friend, Mrs. Green, Mr. J. Gunning, Mr. K. Halls, Mr. T. Harding, Mr. J. Hay, Mr. Lawrence, Miss J. Ledger, Mr. S. Oliver (for the pictures taken from his charity trust collection housed at Royal Holloway College, Egham), Mr. D. Padmore, Mrs. V. Phillips, Mrs. J. Preskett, Mrs. B. Rivett, Mr. E. Roker, Mrs. P. Simmons, Miss K. Trotman, Mr. J. Wetton, Mrs. R. Wilmshurst, Mr. A. White and the Mayford and Woking District History Society and Woking Borough Council. My thanks must also go to Mr. I. J. Christmas, Managing Director of Tavak Ltd. (The Fox Group, Bisley) for allowing me the use of the firm's equipment in preparing this book and for his help in correcting my errors. If any mistakes have slipped through it is not his fault.

Everyone has helped and encouraged me greatly, none more so than my parents, my brother Neil and his wife Tracy, but especially Glenda. I would like to thank her for being so understanding and tolerant whilst I spent long hours working on the final stages of this book.

# PREFACE

Since the publication of my last book, *Bygone Woking*, I have bought, borrowed or been given many old photographs of the borough of Woking. All these old photographs have been copied onto slides, catalogued, and then made available for research. Some have been used in exhibitions, slide shows, or published in local newspapers to help promote interest in Woking's past. As always the wealth of excellent material has made it difficult to decide which pictures to show and which to leave out. Naturally the people of Old Woking would like to see more views of their village, just as those from Brookwood or Byfleet would wish to see more scenes of their areas in the past. I have tried to divide the number of photographs reproduced in this new book equally amongst all the districts based very roughly on their population and size. There are, of course, exceptions to this rule. There are more pictures of Woking town centre, simply because more pictures were taken.

We will never have a complete pictorial record of the borough of Woking, as not every scene has been captured on film. We will never have a complete collection of every picture that was taken, as not all the photographs have survived. But what we can have is a collection of every surviving view of our area, showing part of the Woking of bygone days.

The pictorial record is only a small section of our heritage. Old documents, old artefacts and even old people's memories must also be preserved and made available to us all. In my talks and book I can show part of our collection of old photographs (as well as a small collection of written records, such as the invoices, advertisements etc, included in this volume), but the artefacts and memories are harder to show. I have recorded the recollections of old residents and used this information, but I have not the time to speak to everyone, and whilst the Mayford and Woking District History Society can display a few of the old objects they possess, they have not the room to show them all on a permanent basis. Until Woking gets a museum, all we can do is show part of our past, for part of the time.

With this book, however, we can at least make some of the borough's heritage available to everyone in an easily-accessible and understandable form. Most people now know the basic history of our town. I have, therefore, decided to omit an introduction to local history from this volume, in favour of a couple of sketch maps showing the position of some of the features in the book. Woking is changing rapidly. Even older inhabitants find it hard to remember the location of buildings or roads that no longer exist. The maps will, I hope, help solve the question often asked – 'Where exactly was this picture taken?'. Unfortunately, many more questions must remain unanswered. In most cases it is impossible to place an exact date on the photograph, and we are unable to discover the names of everyone in a school or works group; we cannot always tell the precise location of every scene. But more pictures, more research in old documents and more memories from old people may help to solve some of the questions in the future, and increase our knowledge of Woking's history. If this book has increased your knowledge of Woking, then my task has been worthwhile. If it has increased your desire to know more, then join the Mayford and Woking District History Society, and help campaign for Woking's own museum.

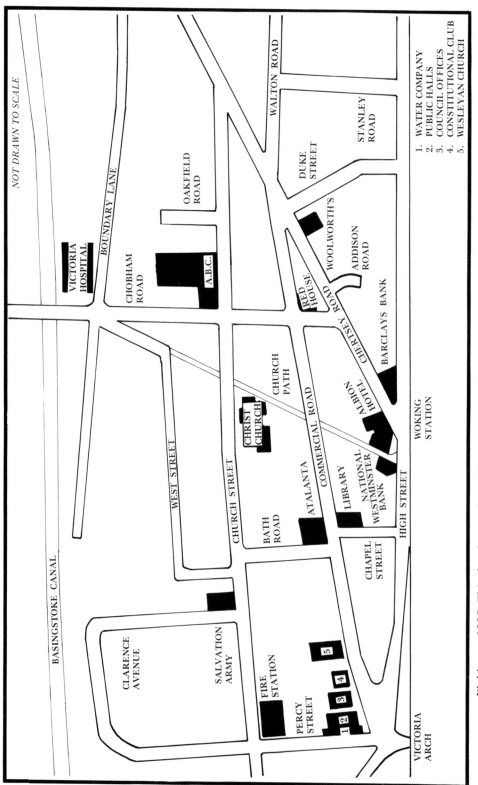

Woking, c. 1937. This sketch map shows Woking as it was before the Second World War. Many old streets have since disappeared or have been divided by modern development. Commercial Road, which once joined Percy Street and Goldsworth Road by Victoria Arch, has now been blocked by the market. At its other end, the Fine Fare supermarket crosses its path and a large area in between has been pedestrianised. Chobham Road has also been cut off to traffic by Victoria Way to the north and between Church Street and Commercial Road. Other roads such as Oakfield Road, Bath Road and Clarence Avenue have been lost completely.

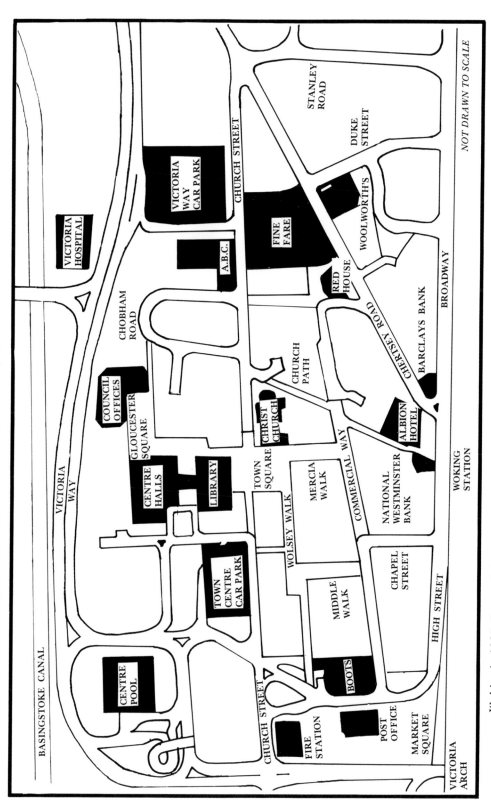

Woking in 1985. Some of the old buildings and sites still remain. Woolworth's, Barclays Bank and the National Westminster Bank still trade from the same sites and the two hotels, the *Albion* and *Red House*, although rebuilt or altered, have not moved from their pre-1939 positions. In Church Street the only building of any age is Christ Church, now surrounded by modern development, whilst on the corner with Chobham Road the former Ritz Cinema can still be found. Woking is changing fast and in another 50 years its appearance may be totally different from how it is today.

*NOT DRAWN TO SCALE*

1. Woking Junction Railway Station. On 21 May 1838 Woking Common Station was opened to the public as the temporary terminus of the London & Southampton Railway. By September the line was complete to Winchfield and by June 1839 trains were running from Nine Elms in London to Basingstoke in Hampshire. Southampton was reached in May 1840, by which time the railway had become the London & South Western Railway. In 1845 the Guildford Branch Railway was built and in 1859, when this line was extended to Havant, Woking became an important railway junction. The excellent train service was a major factor in Woking's development.

2. Jay's carnival van, the Broadway. In the past, Woking celebrated coronations, jubilees, Empire Days, peace celebrations and when it came to raising money for good causes, such as the hospital carnivals of the 1920s and 1930s, the inhabitants would always turn out in force. This picture, taken outside Jay's furnishing stores at No. 11 the Broadway, shows their van ready for the procession around the town.

3. The Broadway, looking from Maybury Road towards the station. The tree on the left marks the boundary of the railway, where the bus shelters are now. Most of the buildings in this picture remain today. Only the two shops on the right, once J. D. Dingle & Co., have been replaced by modern offices. The third shop from the right was The Broadway Tea Rooms and is now the Khyber Pass Restaurant. Hugh Butcher's opened in Woking in 1897 and still occupy the same site.

4. Maybury Road, looking east from Grove Road towards Maybury Arch. Maybury Road, Boundary Road and all the area in between, was originally part of Woking Common, but in the 1870s the London Necropolis & National Mausoleum Company sold the land for development. During the next few decades many houses were built, with most of the larger detached and semi-detached villas nearer to the railway, such as the houses shown here between Grove Road and Portugal Road.

5.  Cecil Terrace, Boundary Road. On 30 June 1907 a terrible storm struck Woking. This shop, on the corner of Boundary Road and Omega Road, was hit by lightning which caused considerable damage. Fortunately no one was killed. The shop is now a hair salon.

6. (*above*) Chertsey Road, looking from the town towards the original Chertsey Road Bridge. Brook House, on the corner of Chertsey Road and Victoria Way, would now be on the left and the Victoria Way roundabout would be in the centre of the picture, with Boundary Road on the right.

7. (*below*) Chertsey Road. Not one of the buildings shown in this picture remains standing today. The shop on the left, on the corner of Chertsey Road and Church Street, was at one time H. J. Ansell, beer retailer and grocer. The shops on the right, including W. J. Singleton, the newsagents, and lower down J. Snowdon, the drapers, have now been replaced by the massive Duke Street development.

"TIPPERARY ROOMS," WOKING.

8.  The Tipperary tea rooms were opened in Duke Street during the First World War to cater for soldiers' wives and children. There was a small play room for the youngsters and a reading room where the ladies could knit clothes for the troops. It is thought that the tea rooms closed soon after the end of the Great War.

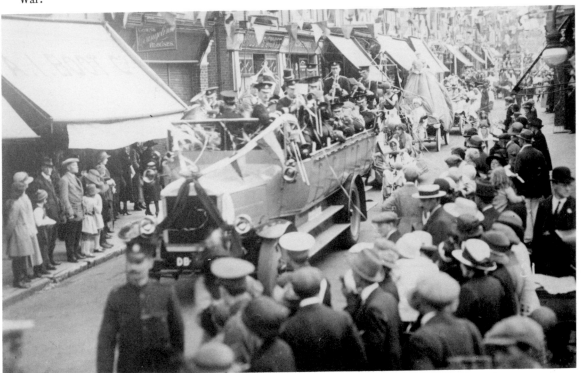

9.  Chertsey Road, the hospital carnival. The carnival of 1923 raised £3,350 towards the rebuilding of the Victoria Cottage Hospital. The total cost of work was about £20,000. Most of the money came from the memorial fund set up after the First World War.

10. (*above*) The right hand side of Chertsey Road, looking from the corner of Duke Street towards the station, has altered beyond recognition. Where Pitcher & Co., the bakers and confectioners, used to trade is now part of the Fine Fare superstore, and even the left hand side of the road has changed, with Woolworth's taking the place of R. & S. Colman's furnishing stores. F. W. Woolworth, Threepenny and Sixpenny Stores, came to Woking in 1926.

11. (*left*) R. & S. Colman advertisement taken from a local guide published in 1913.

Chertsey Road, Woking.

4756-381

12. (*above*) Chertsey Road, looking from Addison Road towards the station. One of the first national companies to start trading in Woking was the International Tea Company Stores Ltd., whose shop can be seen on the left of this picture where Addison Road joins Chertsey Road. The shop is now a hair salon. Other early arrivals to Woking were Freeman, Hardy & Willis, boot stores, and the Home & Colonial Tea Stores, both occupying shops further up the street.

13. (*right*) Notice of opening of the Home & Colonial Tea Stores, printed in 1896.

14. (*above*) Chertsey Road with the original *Red House Hotel* and the junction of Chobham Road on the left. Tibbenham Brothers, on the right, was the first in a series of drapery shops to occupy this site. They were followed by Archibald's, Fairhurst Brothers, Alfred Wyles Ltd. and finally Robinson's, who took over this shop in 1934.

15. (*below*) This photograph of Chertsey Road was probably taken in May 1935 when the Silver Jubilee of King George V was being celebrated. The site of the old *Red House Hotel* is on the far right of the picture. Burton's, the tailors, was built there in 1936. Gloster's Corn Exchange is on the left, with MacFisheries next door, where Barbers Picture Framing shop is now.

16. Chertsey Road, looking in the opposite direction from the previous picture, towards Woking station. We can still see Gloster's Corn Exchange, with the Central Stores and Fred Pullinger's, the bakers, next door. Mr. H. W. Gloster came to Woking in 1875 from Penge. He opened a small shop in Chobham Road called the South Western Stores and was also responsible for the building of the Corn Exchange and Central Stores in Chertsey Road. Later shops were opened at Bagshot and at Kiln Bridge, St John's. The company warehouse was in Commercial Road, behind the Corn Exchange. In 1904 the running of the shops was passed to the managers and Mr. Gloster concentrated on the wholesale side of the business.

17. (*above*) The original *Albion Hotel* was a tall, square, three-storey building erected in 1856-7. It was the first building north of the railway. In the late 1890s it was replaced by a second hotel, which in turn disappeared in the mid-1960s when the present hotel, shops, and office complex was developed by the Norwich Union Insurance Group.

18. (*left*) The High Street, looking from the station towards Chapel Street and Victoria Arch. The development of Woking's shopping centre began in the early 1870s when the shops in the High Street consisted of a carpenter and builder, a draper, a butcher, another carpenter, a grocer and the post office. The post office was opened in 1865 on the corner of the High Street and Church Path. When this photograph was taken, in about 1904, the post office had moved into Chertsey Road and Mr. W. R. Skeet, the ironmonger, occupied the corner shop in the High Street.

19. The High Street, looking from the Broadway. In 1908 Mr. Skeet's shop was sold for £3,300 and the London, County and Westminster Bank was built. It is now the National Westminster Bank. To the right of the bank is the *Albion Hotel*, the second building on this site. The north entrance of the station is on the left.

20. The High Street, looking towards Woking station. Cawsey Way and the market would now be behind the photographer. The tall building on the left, once Emberson's photographic studio, is now March & Stacey's. The shop next door was the Park Farm Dairy, later United Dairies, and is now Mecca, the bookmakers.

21. Empire Day celebration in 1909 in Commercial Road where the market, Cawsey Way and Sparrow Park are now. The photograph was taken from Victoria Arch.

22. This picture was taken exactly 13 years after the one above and shows the unveiling of the war memorial at Sparrow Park by Field Marshal Sir William Robertson, Bart., on 24 May 1922. The war memorial was moved to its present site in the Town Square early in 1975.

23. Commercial Road from the air. Only the High Street shops at the bottom right of the picture have survived. Commercial Road (crossing from bottom left to middle right) has changed completely. Boots would now be in the centre of the picture, where the Wesleyan chapel once stood. Cawsey Way cuts through the Constitutional Club next door, and the old council offices and Water Company offices have been replaced by the post office and Premier House. The houses of Church Street can be seen behind the Wesleyan church with Clarence Avenue and West Street just visible in the distance.

24. (*above*) On the corner of Commercial Road and Bath Road was the Y.M.C.A. head-quarters. This photograph, taken in May 1916, shows their flag day. Troops waiting to return to the war are standing outside the hall, which later became the Atalanta Ballroom.

25. (*below*) In January 1935 Woking Urban District Council decided to demolish houses in Commercial Road to make way for a car park. The houses from Church Path to the Atalanta Ballroom were pulled down in 1936-7, with the car park being opened just before Christmas 1937. This photograph shows the demolition of Nos. 17-31 Commercial Road in 1936. During the 1970s this site was developed as part of Woking's new town centre.

26. In the redevelopment of Woking, whole roads have disappeared. The section of Commercial Road shown in this picture has been replaced by part of the Fine Fare super-store. The view today, taken from opposite the *Red House Hotel*, would merely show Crown Square and the entrance to Fine Fare's store.

27. Chobham Road, looking from Chertsey Road towards the junction with Commercial Road. The *Red House Hotel* is on the right with J. Wearing's chemist shop on the corner where Crown House is now. Meek's, on the left, began business in Woking in 1890 and now trade from premises further down Chobham Road.

28.  Chobham Road. Crown House has replaced all the buildings on the right from Wearing's on the corner with Commercial Road to Skeet & Jeffes at the junction of Church Street. The shops opposite were demolished and replaced by British Home Stores. The Woking Electric Supply Company, whose showrooms are on the right, were formed in 1889 with their works being built and operated by New & Mayne in Board School Road. Power was first supplied to the Woking area in 1890.

29.  The Ritz Cinema on the corner of Church Street and Chobham Road. Once Woking had three cinemas. The Ritz, or A.B.C. Cinema as it later became known, was built in 1937. It was the last to be opened and the last to close. Woking's other cinemas were the Central Halls (or Plaza or Gaumont) in Chertsey Road next to the *Woking News & Mail* offices, and the Palace (or Astoria or Odeon) in Duke Street on the corner with the Broadway.

30.  Chobham Road, looking towards the shops of Chertsey Road which are just visible in the background. Only two of the four shops with gabled roofs on the right of this picture remain today. They are S. K. Radio and Horace Smith, the locksmith. The other two were demolished and replaced by Heater's the bakers, and the link road from Church Street and West Street. The Central Buildings were built on the land to the right during the 1930s.

WHEATSHEAF BRIDGE & COTTAGE HOSPITAL, WOKING

31.  The Victoria Cottage Hospital, looking from the Horsell side of the canal with the shops of Chobham Road on the far right of the picture. Woking's first hospital opened in 1893 in Bath Road when a house was converted into the Woking, Horsell and Woodham Cottage Hospital. In 1897 work began on a new hospital by Wheatsheaf Bridge to commemorate the Diamond Jubilee of Queen Victoria. The Victoria Cottage Hospital was opened in 1899 at a cost of £4,200.

CHRIST CHURCH WOKING

32. (*left*) Christ Church, now the only old building in Church Street, was begun in 1887. The building itself has remained almost unaltered but its surroundings have drastically changed. New shops and offices, a road and a square have been built around the church and the well-trimmed hedge has been replaced by a wall.

33. (*below*) The Salvation Army Hall, on the corner of Church Street and Clarence Avenue, was built in 1910 at a cost of £1,528. The Woking Corps was formed in October 1897 when a travelling 'cavalry van' came to the town to gain new members. The early years were not easy for the Army's followers. In 1901 Woking's Captain Prestage was arrested for holding an open air meeting on the corner of Chertsey Road and Commercial Road. He was fined one pound but refused to pay and, when the police tried to distrain his goods to cover the costs, he gave all his possessions away. In the end he was sentenced to imprisonment at Wandsworth and on his release was drawn through the streets of Woking in a wagon dressed in his prison clothes. The new Salvation Army Hall, in Walton Road, was built in 1972 and cost £35,000.

GOLDSWORTH ROAD, WOKING.

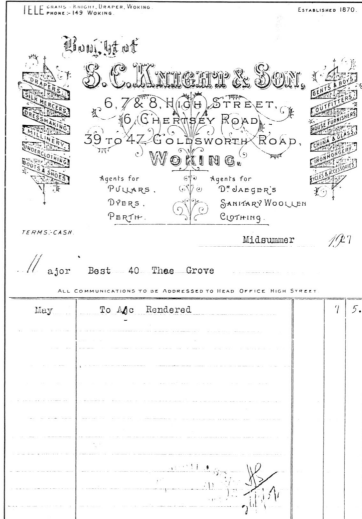

34. (*above*) Goldsworth Road, looking towards the junction with Church Street. The shops on the right have remained more or less the same whilst the buildings on the left have disappeared under yet more offices. S. C. Knight's shops on the right sold everything from cycles (in the shop on the corner with Church Street), to boots, ironmongery, china and glass, with house furnishings in the shops nearest the photographer. This later became John Perring's furniture shop.

35. (*right*) Invoice sent from S. C. Knight & Son to Major Best of The Grove, Horsell, in 1927.

Goldsworth Road. Woking.

W.H.A.3721.

36. (*above*) Only a few of these old shops in Goldsworth Road still survive. The buildings from the World's Stores on the left to G. Chandler's Printing Works have now been demolished. The shop to the right of Chandler's, now without its bay windows, is Continental Motors. The brick wall and hedge on the right of the picture have gone and the land has been used for shops and offices.

37. (*below*) Goldsworth Road, from the junction of the Kingsway with the offices and chapels of the Woking Funeral Service (incorporating H. Ingram and A. D. Lamdin) on the left. The *Goldsworth Arms* public house is on the right. The Ingram family came to Woking in 1874 from Cowes on the Isle of Wight. Mr. Ingram was employed installing water tanks at Woking station. He liked the area and in 1880 began a building and contracting business in Goldsworth Road. In 1916 his son James Henry Ingram took over the firm and was later joined by his sons. Gradually undertaking replaced the building work.

38. (*above*) The Triangle, taken from the railway arch, showing the lane to St John's Road on the left. Triggs Lane is on the right, heading towards Goldsworth Road where the round-about and entrance to Goldsworth Park are now.

39. (*below*) St John's Road, looking towards the village centre with the grounds of the *Rowbarge* on the right. George Kingham's tailor shop is on the corner behind the public house sign. Further along the road was Mrs. Battrick, bootmaker, and George Griffith, outfitter.

40. (*left*) The old *Rowbarge*, beside the Basingstoke Canal, was once a popular haunt of boatmen who could moor their barges below lock 11 and walk down the lane to the bar. It is said that two Tudor cottages once stood on this site, one of which was the village bakery.

41. (*below*) St John's Wesleyan chapel. On the corner of St John's Road and St John's Hill Road was the Wesleyan chapel which was later converted into a garage and is now Phipps Motors. This old photograph, taken in the late 1890s, shows one of the very popular church or Sunday School outings.

The Schools, St. Johns, Woking

Southern Series E

42. On the corner of Church Road and St John's Hill Road, where Scylla and Apollo Place is now, was St John's Church School, built in the mid-1850s. It was enlarged in 1869 and again in 1877 after the Woking School Board took over responsibility for the buildings. A report of 1907 states that the school was 'awkwardly arranged' and that there were 'no means of artificially lighting the school beyond oil lamps [although] gas and electric mains pass the building'. The ventilation was not satisfactory, the heating was poor and the floor was worn.

43. This unusual scene shows the back of St John's church with the cottage and grounds of St John's Nursery in the foreground. The view was taken from near the footbridge over the railway, on the path to Woking Golf Club.

44. An advertisement for Woking's Dairies, taken from a local guide published in 1924.

45.  The 60 acres of St John's Lye were excluded from the sale of common land to the London Necropolis & National Mausoleum Company in 1854, following pressure from the Vicar of Woking. He wanted the land to be kept for the people of Woking, who were to be allowed to exercise their common rights and use the Lye for recreation. Although common rights no longer apply, the Lye is still open to the public thanks to the Rev. Charles Bradshaw Bowles.

46.  Kiln Bridge was one of the first bridges over the Basingstoke Canal to be rebuilt. The original structure, like all the others, was a brick arch built in the 1790s but in 1898 the Woking, Aldershot and Basingstoke Canal and Navigation Co. Ltd. wrote to Woking Council proposing to knock down the old bridge. They knew that the council wanted to widen the carriageway from 15 ft. to 30 ft. and so they offered to pull down their arch and rebuild foundations suitable for an iron-girder bridge. Woking Urban District Council was to provide and maintain the new structure and in 1899 the Kiln Bridge was built.

47. Kiln Bridge and St John's Road. The buildings in this part of St John's are still more or less the same as in this photograph. Framichel Gift Shop, by Kiln Bridge, was H. Trump's, drapers and milliners, whose painted sign can still be seen on the other side of the building. Opposite, where the bus shelter is now, was the old village fire station. It was opened in 1895 with just four men and equipment, including a 30 ft. ladder, two short ladders and a jumping sheet.

48. St John's welcomes the Duchess of Albany. In 1907 the Duchess of Albany, of Claremont House, Esher, visited Woking to lay the foundation stone of the new Holy Trinity church at Knaphill. The route took her through St John's where the traders and villagers came out to welcome her and cheer her on her way.

49. View from Prince Hill. The cottages of Copse Road on the right and the houses of Robin Hood Road on the left are still standing today. The land in the foreground, at one time a sandpit, has since been built on. The Basingstoke Canal and Kiln Bridge would be behind the photographer, with the *Prince of Wales* public house (which closed in 1984) to his left.

50. On the corner of Robin Hood Road, Hermitage Road and Barrack Path was Daphne Cottage, now the veterinary surgery. Next door to the cottage, along Robin Hood Road, was the St John's Garage where the open-top double decker bus of the Mills bus service can be seen. Mr. Frank Mills is leaning on another of his vehicles in the centre of the picture.

Hermitage Road, (St. Johns End,) Woking.                    Southern Series. 8.0.

51. (*above*) Hermitage Road, looking from the junction with Barrack Path and Robin
Hood Road towards the houses of Temple Bar in the background. These have now been
replaced by the Health Centre. The shops of Graphic House have replaced Henry Tyler,
baker and confectioner, on the right and the canal-side car park has been constructed
between the buildings on the left and Temple Bar.

52. (*below*) Another of Mr. Mills's buses is shown here outside his garage in Hermitage
Road, where Kiln Bridge House is now. The Mills family were connected with several
businesses in the village. As well as the garages and bus service, there was also a small
milliner's shop in Hermitage Road run by Frank Mills's daughters.

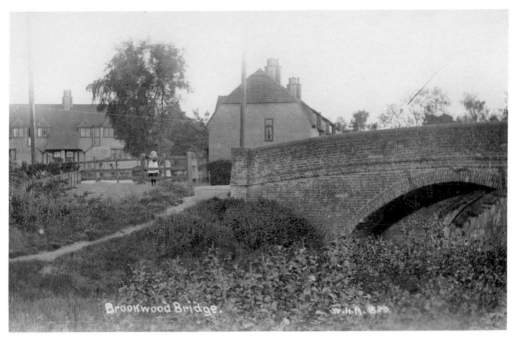

Brookwood Bridge.
W.H.A. 1529.

53. Stumps Bridge. In the early part of this century most of the canal bridges in the Woking area were falling into decay. Hermitage Bridge collapsed in 1906 when a traction engine carrying potatoes to Inkerman Barracks fell through and in 1914 the old Stumps Bridge by Brookwood crossroads also had to be replaced. Woking Urban District Council carried out the repairs and then tried to recover the costs from the owners of the canal, but despite winning the case they never received any money.

PIRBRIGHT BRIDGE & LOCK. WOKING. 702.

54. Lock 15 on the Basingstoke Canal taken from Pirbright Bridge with the railway bridge to Bisley camp in the background. The line to the National Rifle Association's ranges was constructed in 1890 when the N.R.A. moved from Wimbledon to Bisley. The bridge over the canal was built by Royal Engineers from Aldershot with the assistance of the London & South Western Railway Co., which provided rail facilities and contributed £1,000 towards its cost. They also enlarged Brookwood station. The railway bridge no longer remains but the lock has been restored by the Surrey & Hampshire Canal Society.

55.  Taken in the early years of this century, this view of Connaught Road looking east towards the village centre illustrates how little Brookwood has changed over the years. The houses are still standing; only the condition of the road has changed.

56.  Brookwood station. The London & Southampton Railway was opened to Woking in 1838 and to Basingstoke a year later but the station at Brookwood was not built until 1864. In the meantime, the London Necropolis & National Mausoleum Co. had built their branch railway into Brookwood cemetery in 1854, where two stations served both the north and south sections. When the main line station was opened Brookwood village began to expand.

57. One of the first places to be built after the main line station opened was the *Brookwood Hotel* which still stands almost opposite the north entrance to the station.

58. Connaught Road. The shop on the left was the village post office run by Mr. C. W. Blackaby. It was Mr. Blackaby who was responsible for the formation of the Brookwood volunteer fire brigade in 1906. This was taken over by the council brigade in 1912.

59. (*above*) Connaught Road. The exit from Brookwood station is on the right of this picture as we look from the post office towards Brookwood crossroads. More houses have been built on the common land beyond the villas to the left.

60. (*left*) This rare old photograph shows the interior of the original telephone exchange at Brookwood. It was opened in the 1920s in a house in Connaught Villas, shown on the right of the picture above.

THE PRINCESS CHRISTIAN HOME

61.  On the border of Knaphill and Bisley, at Stafford Lake, is the Princess Christian Home for disabled soldiers, sailors and airmen. The Home was built in 1900 on land given by Lord Pirbright. This photograph was taken soon after its opening.

62. The Upper Guildford Road, or Chobham Road as it is now known, has changed considerably since the days of pony and traps. However, nearly all the old houses in this picture still remain today with the addition of modern houses where the trees once stood.

63. Chobham Road. The houses and outbuildings in this picture still survive today. Stanley Farm was owned by Mr. D. Stevens, whose horse and removal cart can be seen in this picture. One of his sons was employed carting coal from Brookwood station to Brookwood Hospital, whilst another ran the farm. The cart in the picture is believed to survive still, rotting away in a Bisley orchard.

64. High Street. The church school at Knaphill, built in the 1860s, was taken over by the Woking School Board in 1877. A new school was built in 1880-1 for £2,090. The old school building shown here was demolished in the summer of 1983.

65. The High Street has altered almost beyond recognition since this photograph was taken. The main landmark, the *Crown* public house on the left, can still be seen on the corner with Highclere Road, but the land on either side has now been replaced by shops. To the right of the *Crown* was once an orchard where apple and hazel trees grew. Most of the shops on the right of this picture still stand with some modern additions. The shop in the distance was once the village post office, but has now been replaced by the Co-operative supermarket.

66.  W. Johnson's greengrocery and fruit shop in the High Street, now occupied by
Knaphill Butchers.

67.  This view of the High Street and the Broadway shows William Ruglys, newsagents, stationers and drapers on the left, where Boorman's the jewellers and Broadway Fabrics are now. The High Street turns to the right with the Broadway to the left. At the junction of the two roads, once overgrown with trees, the second branch of the Woking and Horsell Co-operative Society was built. It was opened on 6 July 1913. Mann & Co., estate agents, are now on this site.

68.  The Broadway, looking towards the High Street. This postcard was published by Chris Trusler, whose shop can be seen to the right, on the corner with Queen's Road.

69. Brookwood Hospital from the air. In the top right hand corner of this picture can be seen part of Inkerman Barracks (formerly the Women's Convict Prison) and in the top left is the village of Knaphill. The Surrey county justices purchased the 150 acres of land for Brookwood Hospital in 1860 for £10,500. By 1881 the total cost of construction had reached £104,855 17s. 1d.

70. Inkerman Barracks from the air. The Male Convict Prison between Knaphill and St John's was converted in 1895 into Inkerman Barracks and in 1899 the Female Prison (on the left of this picture) was also transferred from the Home Office to the War Department. The buildings remained in military use until 1965 when Inkerman Barracks closed. The former officers' quarters along Barrack Path (crossing the centre of the picture) have since been converted into private homes. A new housing estate has replaced the original prison buildings.

71.  Knaphill brickworks. There had been brickworks in this area for centuries, but it was not until the 1880s that production reached its peak, with many bricks being used in the houses of the fast-growing town of Woking. In the 1790s the brick kilns of St John's had helped in the making of the Basingstoke Canal and in the 1860s Knaphill's brickfields produced the raw materials for the nearby prison and asylum. In the 1851 census there were 21 brickmakers in Woking and by 1921 the total had reached 44, but in 1925 the Anchor Hill Brickworks, shown here, closed and by 1942 all brick production in this area had ceased.

72.  The *Barley Mow* public house, now a private home on the corner of Barley Mow Lane and Chobham Road, was built in the 17th century. It was a hunting lodge for Windsor forest during the reign of Charles I and became a public house in the 19th century. At about this time it was sold, together with the *Sun Inn* at Chobham and 340 acres of land, for just £350. The licence of the *Barley Mow* was given up in 1921 and the old inn was converted into a private house by Mr. H. P. Lawson. Legend records that a soldier was murdered outside the building in 1816 and that his ghost still appears, holding his head underneath his arm.

73. Knaphill Nursery, the rhododendron walk. Knaphill Nursery was established by Michael Waterer in 1795. In 1828 a second Michael Waterer took over and in 1844 it passed to his son, Horsea. In the 1870s Anthony Waterer was the owner. One of his apprentices was Walter Slocock who in 1877 acquired Goldsworth Nursery. Nearly one hundred years later his grandson, Martin, was forced to sell this nursery when Goldsworth Park was developed. In 1976 Martin Slocock moved to Knaphill, to carry on business, where his grandfather had learned his trade.

74. Blewgates (or Bluegates) corner at Lower Knaphill where Barrs Lane joins the Littlewick Road. The house on the corner of Barrs Lane is called 'Inwoods' and dates from the 16th century. It is a grade II listed building. Further along Littlewick Road, behind the horse and cart, can be seen the buildings of Whitfield Court, another 16th-century grade II listed house.

75. Cheapside, looking from South Road towards the corner of Horsell Rise and Cheapside. On the corner is the Horsell Common Baptist chapel built in 1811 and restored in 1907. The common land opposite has since become overgrown with trees but the houses and cottages of Cheapside remain more or less the same.

76. The forge, Cheapside. In the past almost every village had its own blacksmith's forge. In Knaphill there was a blacksmith's and wheelwright's workshop in Robin Hood Road. In Old Woking H. Bedford had his forge in the High Street, and in Horsell there was Henry Ellis's smithy and wheelwright's shop at Cheapside. The long, low building in the picture housed the forge, with a small shop in the building next door. The forge no longer remains; houses have been built on the site, but its existence is recorded in the house named 'Forge End'.

*Horsell Foot Beagles, 1907.*

77. Formed originally as the Chertsey Beagles and kennelled in the town, the Horsell Foot Beagles were acquired in 1874 by Mr. Bailey and from 1889 were housed at Scotchers Farm or at Sheerwater Court. By 1896 they had become known as the Horsell Foot Beagles and were kennelled at Cheapside, but in 1919 they became the West Surrey and Horsell Beagles. The exact location of this photograph is as yet uncertain.

## WEST SURREY AND HORSELL BEAGLES.

THE

# Hunt Dinner and Dance

WILL BE HELD AT

## NUTHALL'S RESTAURANT,

KINGSTON - ON - THAMES,

ON

### FRIDAY, JANUARY 20th, 1922,

AT **7 p.m**

TICKETS, including Dinner and Dance, **£1 1s. 0d.** (exclusive of Wines).

Private Tables will be arranged for parties of six and upwards.

Application for Tickets should be made to the Hon. Dance Secretary,

'Phone : ESHER 115.  A. CLOWES,

PEAR TREE COTTAGE,

CARRIAGES **1 a.m.**  CLAYGATE, SURREY.

78.  West Surrey & Horsell Beagles. Notice of Hunt Dinner and Dance printed in 1922.

79.  Ebenezer Cottage, *c*. 1929. On the corner of the High Street and South Road was Ebenezer Cottage, the grounds of which extended along the High Street to Thornash Road. The cottage stood next to the bakery, where Modplas Ltd. are now. The old loading gantry for the sacks of flour can be seen in the background to the right of the chimney.

80. Horsell High Street, looking from the corner of Nursery Road towards the village centre. The houses on the left still stand, as do the older buildings in the distance, near the junction with Ormonde Road. The land on the right was part of James Cobbett & Sons Nursery, which began in the 1840s and closed in 1938 when Mr. H. Crane of Thornash Road built the houses of the Horsell High Street Estate on the land.

High St. Horsell.

81. High Street. The village centre of Horsell has altered completely, with modern shops being built where fields were once grazed by sheep and cattle. The old barn in this picture, next to Benstead's Garage, no longer remains and the rural appearance of Horsell has been lost forever.

82. Canon Pares, in the centre of the photograph, standing by the door of the caravan, was vicar of Horsell from 1897 to 1935. This picture was taken outside the parish hall when a touring mission visited the area to help promote the church, *c.* 1930.

83. Horsell church. The oldest part of St Mary's church probably dates from the 12th century when the first stone chapel is thought to have been built on this site. It was rebuilt in the 14th century with the south aisle being added in the 15th century. The earliest recorded burial in Horsell's churchyard also dates from the 15th century and there are still many old tombs and gravestones dating from the 18th century which commemorate local families. The church tower has been restored many times since it was first built in the 14th century. In 1884 it was encased in chalk stone which cost £1,226, but by 1932 this was showing signs of decay and was removed.

84. Church Hill, looking from the church towards the junction of Waldens Park Road on the right. The cows being herded up the hill illustrate how rural parts of Woking were in the early years of this century. The name Horsell is thought to have derived from the Old English 'horig', meaning foul or dirty, and 'scylf', meaning slope or shelf. It is perhaps easy to imagine this 'dirty hill' in the days before tarmacadamed roads.

85. Abbey Road, looking from Well Lane towards Arthur's Bridge Road. Abbey Farm was sold in 1890 and developed in two stages during 1892 and 1896. The road was made up by Woking Urban District Council in 1911.

86.  The Rose Cottage Laundry, near Step Bridge, was owned by Mr. Edgar Ashley Cook in 1916. It was a small family firm with many employees starting straight from school and sometimes whole families worked there together. Most of the staff were female with just a few male drivers and supervisors.

87. Chobham Road. The *Wheatsheaf Hotel* is on the left, with the recreation ground opposite. The houses of Ferndale Road can be seen on the edge of the Wheatsheaf recreation ground and in the distance is Woking town.

88. Gipsies in the pines. For centuries gipsies have camped on the commons and heathland around Woking, moving on whenever they wanted or when forced to by local residents. There were no special sites in the old days; the horse-drawn caravans would stop in the trees and the washing would dry in the bushes.

"The Bleak House," Horsell, Woking.     E. Bennett, Proprietor.

89.   The *Bleak House Inn*, at St Anthony's, Horsell Common, has changed considerably since this photograph was taken. An extension has been built on the area once enclosed by the wooden fence and the car park occupies the land to the right.

90.   Monument Bridge, or Bunkers Bridge as it was originally known, looking from the Sheerwater side, with the trees of Horsell Common in the background. During the late 1930s Woking Urban District Council decided to rebuild Monument Bridge. In July 1937 it estimated that replacement of the bridge would cost £8,941 but by October this had increased to £9,064. Its final cost was £12,780, with half the money coming in the form of a grant from the Ministry of Transport.

91.   Woodhambury, Woodham Road, was built in 1889 by Mr. W. F. Unsworth, who designed
All Saints' Church, Woodham, and Christ Church in Woking. In *Bygone Woking* a postcard
entitled 'Woodham Hall' was included, but this was in fact a picture of Woodhambury.

92.   Lock 2, Scotland Lock.
The canal was opened in the
early 1790s to carry agricul-
tural goods from the towns
and villages of Surrey and
Hampshire to London, with
coal and consumable goods
on the return journey. In the
early days of this century
horse-drawn barges could be
seen quite often but in 1921
trade above Horsell ceased
and in 1936 the last load of
coal was carried for the gas
works at Woking. The year
1949 witnessed the last boat
laden with timber and gradually the canal became derelict.
Now, however, the Surrey
and Hampshire Canal Society
are working hard on its restoration which will, it is
hoped, be finished in the very
near future.

Scotland Lock
West Byfleet. 8.

93. Camphill Road with the narrow 18th-century Scotland Bridge in the background. The photograph, taken in the early years of this century, shows a group of workmen repairing the footpath outside York Cottages. The cottages still remain, as does the bridge, but the land to the right of the road has been developed with factories, and the rural appearance of Camphill Road has been lost.

94. Station Road, looking west towards the station. This old postcard is a reminder of the days when most of the roads were mere dirt tracks and when milk was not delivered to doorsteps in bottles, but carried in churns on hand carts or horse-drawn floats to every street. When the milk cart arrived the housewives would bring out their own jugs for the milkman to fill. It was not until the 1920s that milk began to be bottled.

95. Birchwood Road was built by the Birchwood Tenant Company, which was owned by Mr. F. C. Stoop of West Hall. The houses were thought to have been built by Mr. W. G. Tarrant of Byfleet. The road was opened by the Labour M.P. Mr. Tommy Burns on 13 May 1911.

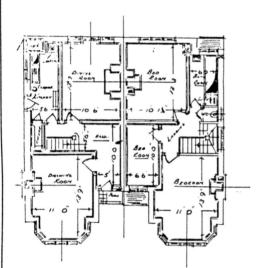

*Ideal Houses in an Ideal Setting
Ideally Planned*

# SHEERWATER ESTATE
## WEST BYFLEET

(Two Minutes from Station)

*Situated amongst glorious sur-
roundings in beautiful Surrey*

## SUPERB HOUSES
# From £625

FREEHOLD, NO ROAD OR PAVING
CHARGES, NO LEGAL FEES, AND
SPACE FOR GARAGE

**Weekly Repayments 17/3 per week**

# NO EXTRAS WHATSOEVER

Please forward one of your illustrated
Booklets

Name ...........................................................................

Address ........................................................................

........................................................................
WR.

# E. THOMAS & Co.

*Sheerwater Estate*
**WEST BYFLEET**

Phone : BYFLEET 645.

96.   Sheerwater Estate. Advertisement taken from the local newspaper, published in 1933.

97. West Byfleet station. In 1884 the London and South Western Railway Company agreed to build a station to serve the communities of Byfleet, Woodham and Pyrford. It considered sites at Camphill Road and Sheerwater Road before finally deciding on a site between the two at Byfleet Corner. The station was opened in 1887 and called Byfleet and Woodham station.

98. Station Approach with Barclays Bank in the background. The house and trees to the right, on the corner with Madeira Road, have been replaced by a new office block called West Lodge. The Sheer House Shopping Centre has been built on the land opposite. The shop on the left, formerly Robert Wasley's, is still a butcher's, now called F. A. Brookes.

99.   The Old Woking Road, looking from West Byfleet. Many of the large
houses along the road were built in the late 19th or early 20th century. The
area to the south, over Coldharbour, was developed after the Second World
War, when the 600 houses of the Pyrford Woods Estate were built.

100.   This rare old postcard shows the Byfleet Automobile Engineering Co. Garage on the corner
of Rosemount Avenue and the Old Woking Road, where the launderette is now. The garage was the
sole agent in this area for B.S.A. cars as well as supplying other items needed by the pioneer motor-
ists of Woking.

101. Madeira Road, looking from Camphill Road. The houses in this section of Madeira Road have, on the whole, managed to survive redevelopment, unlike those nearer to Sheerwater Road, many of which have been replaced by modern houses and flats. All the houses in this photograph remain today.

102. The large and impressive West Hall, near the Wey Navigation at West Byfleet, was once the home of the Stoop family which contributed greatly to village life in the late 19th and early 20th centuries. Mr. F. C. Stoop paid for the construction of the village hall in 1898 to celebrate the Diamond Jubilee of Queen Victoria.

103. (*above*) The Wey Navigation at Byfleet, looking downstream towards Parvis Bridge. If the picture was taken today, the new bridge which crosses the Navigation and M25 would be directly above the photographer. The building on the right still remains and boats can still be hired from the Byfleet Boat Club on the other side of the old bridge.

104. (*below*) The entrance to Byfleet village from Parvis Bridge has changed dramatically. Parvis Road now takes the main traffic away from the village centre and would be on the left of this view today.

105.  The *Queen's Head* may once have been known as the *Leather Bottle*, as a public house of that name was recorded on or near this site between 1847 and 1860. It was owned by Mr. Henry Dennett, of the Byfleet Brewery, with Mr. George Chuter as the tenant. Mr. Chuter was later recorded as the landlord of the *Queen's Head*. George Chuter was born in Byfleet in July 1820 and lived in the area all his life. His brutal murder on 12 March 1888 at his cottage in Chertsey Road caused quite a stir in the village. Three days after the murder a public meeting in the village hall was attended by 150 people who promised to give £100 to anyone giving information leading to the capture of the murderer. Unfortunately he was never found.

714. Byfleet. Entrance to the Village.

106. (*above*) High Road, looking towards the junction with Chertsey Road. The tall building in the centre of the picture belonged to Lloyd Derisley who came originally from Diss in Norfolk but in the 1870s moved to Wisley to help his brother, Robert, at Church Farm. In the 1880s Lloyd began his own business as a butcher and in 1894 built this north-facing shop in the High Road, Byfleet.

107. (*below*) High Road, looking towards the *Plough Inn* and the junction with Oyster Lane. The shops on the right still stand but the wooden fence and hedge of Royston Place have long since gone. 'Byfleet Green', outside Lipton's supermarket, would now be on the left, with Royston Avenue just behind the photographer. The *Plough Inn* was originally next to Plough Bridge. It was frequently flooded, so in 1847 it was pulled down and moved to a drier site in the centre of the village.

High Road, Byfleet.

W.HA.2111.

HIGH ROAD, BYFLEET.

108. High Road, taken from where Chuter Close is now, looking towards the post office. More shops have been built on the land to the left of the post office and the Blue Star Garage would now be on the left of the picture. B. & W. Denley's, the tobacconist and confectioner's on the right of the picture, also served teas and light refreshments. The building still remains as does the post office further along the road.

109. High Road, looking towards the junction with Brewery Lane, with the post office now on the left of the picture and B. & W. Denley's shop in the distance.

110.   The Clock House, near the corner of Church Road and the High Road, was once known as Byfleet Lodge.
The Clock House was taken over by the Fellowship Trust in 1948 for conversion into flats for elderly people.
This is a view of the back garden and lake taken in the early part of this century.

Weybridge Motor Track. "The Subway."

111. (*above*) The track of Brooklands was designed by Colonel H. C. L. Holden, R.E., for Mr. Hugh Fortescue Locke-King. Work began in autumn 1906 and involved the cutting of 30 acres of woodland as well as diverting the river Wey in two places. The track was opened in July 1907.

112. (*below*) The opening ceremony of Brooklands track. Before the track was officially opened, Mr. S. F. Edge established a new 24-hour record by travelling around the track at an average of 65.9 m.p.h. The world record attempt, on 28 and 29 June 1907, caused much trouble for Mr. Locke-King. The concrete track was found to be breaking up and local residents complained of the terrible noise. Byfleet still has a noisy, cracked concrete 'race track'—the M25.

Plough Bridges, Byfleet.

W.H.A. 3983.

113.  After severe flooding in February 1900, when Plough Bridge gave way and became impassable for several days, Chertsey Rural District Council decided that the bridge must be rebuilt. The cost of repairs during 1903-4 came to £1,700.

Byfleet Mill and Mill House.

114.  Byfleet Mill and Mill House. The 18th-century weatherboarded mill stands on a site recorded in the Domesday Book of 1086. By about 1670 Byfleet Mill was producing paper and, when William Sutton rebuilt it in 1687, it was described as a 'white paper mill'. In 1703 the mill was making iron. Steel was produced in 1794 but it later reverted to corn, under the ownership of the Holroyd family. The mill house was built in about 1750.

115.  The manor of Byfleet was granted to Chertsey Abbey in A.D. 673 and was held by Ulwin, a tenant of the abbey, at the time of the Domesday survey. Between 1297 and 1315 it passed to King Edward II, who granted it to Piers Gaveston. In 1326 the manor became part of the duchy of Cornwall, but in 1533 it was granted to Catherine of Aragon on her divorce from Henry VIII. When she died in 1536 it passed back into royal hands. In the 1540s Sir Anthony Browne was responsible for the demolition of the old medieval house and the building of a new manor house. Various owners have since rebuilt or repaired the house. Anne, wife of James I, began reconstruction in 1615, which was completed by Sir Thomas Fullerton in the 1620s, and in the late 17th century the house was again rebuilt as it was said to be too large.

116.  Byfleet Parish Day began in June 1865 as a celebration of the restoration of St Mary's church. Up to 1885 it was always held on 1 June, but after that date it was held on various days during July. In 1888 it included a flower show, sports, dancing, and a band. In 1892 there was a cycle race through the grounds of West Hall and in 1895 the local fire brigade gave a display. It is uncertain where or when this photograph was taken.

117. Pyrford Lock, looking downstream, with the original *Anchor* public house in the background. The bar of the *Anchor* was in the cottage kitchen. The present public house was built in 1934.

118. The ford at Pyrford with St Nicholas church on the hill in the background. The name Pyrford means 'the ford by a pear tree' and was first recorded in A.D. 698. The church dates from the 12th century and is most famous for its wall paintings which date from Norman times.

119.   The St Nicholas Home for crippled children at Pyrford was built in 1906 on land bought by Mr. F. C. Stoop of West Hall. The school within the home was founded in 1918.

120.  This old photograph of the Sonnes family of Old Woking was taken at Pyrford and shows the ancient Pyrford Stone, which now stands at the entrance to Pyrford Court. A legend attached to the stone recalls that every night, when the clock of St Nicholas's church strikes twelve, the stone will turn.  This might be credible if it were not for the fact that St Nicholas's church has never had a clock.

South West Wing, St. Peter's Convent, Woking.

121. (*above*) The St Peter's Convent at Maybury was built in 1883 to provide a home 'for such of the sick poor as are members of the Church of England and require nursing'. It is a grade II listed building.

122. (*below*) The verandah of the Lancaster Ward, St Peter's Convent. Mr. Benjamin Lancaster was a London businessman and governor of St George's Hospital. In 1861 he founded the community of St Peter in a house in Brompton Square where discharged patients could convalesce. In 1869 the home moved to Kilburn and in 1883 Mr. Lancaster paid for the construction of the St Peter's Home at Maybury. The buildings were designed by Mr. J. L. Pearson who is perhaps most famous for his work in building Truro Cathedral.

Verandah of Lancaster Ward, St. Peter's Home, Woking.

123.   In the past almost every village had its own dairy. In St John's there was J. C. Renshaw's Dairy, established in 1870. Horsell had J. Holmes & Sons 'model dairy', with milk from Birch and Wapshot Farms, and in Old Woking and Pyrford there was the Guinness Dairy. This picture, taken in about 1923 at Frailey Hill, shows one of the carts owned by the Guinness Dairy of Hoe Bridge Farm.

124. This photograph is looking down Maybury Hill with College Road on the right. Tony Brooks's Garage would occupy the shop on the corner. In the distance is Maybury Arch and on the left, by the lamp post, is Oriental Road. The Oriental Institute, from which the road gets its name, was opened in 1884 and closed in 1899. Part of the building still survives in the factory of James Walker's, whose boardroom is housed in the remains of the old central hall of the Institute.

125. St Paul's church. In 1884 the ancient parish of St Peter's, Old Woking, was divided into two when the parish of St John's was formed. This in turn was also subdivided in 1893 with the building of Christ Church and just two years later the chapel of ease at Maybury was built. The need for more churches and smaller parishes in the last 100 years is a good example of the rate of growth in the Woking area during the late 19th and 20th centuries.

126.   The Southern Railway Orphanage was built in 1909. The railway line can be seen at the top of the photograph, with Oriental Road running across the centre. The Home was extended soon after this photograph was taken. A new wing, facing Oriental Road, was opened in 1935.

127.   Danes Hill, Hockering. In 1904 the 130-acre Hockering Estate was laid out with four roads known later as Cleardown, Danes Hill, Hockering Road, and Knowl Hill. The estate was developed by the Smallpiece family of Kingfield House, who originally came from the small village of Hockering, Norfolk. Most of the houses date from after the First World War.

128.   White Rose Farm, a grade II listed building, was built in the 16th century as a hall house. Its barn dates from the early 19th century and the small granary from the 18th century. In 1548 it is recorded as being called 'Whitetrowes', which probably derives from the Old English word 'treow' meaning tree.

129. (*left*) Lovers' Walk, White Rose Lane. The footpath from Maybury to Old Woking descends the hill from Heathfield Road by a steep path known to many as the Jack and Jill steps. When this photograph was taken, however, it was known as Lovers' Walk.

130. (*below*) From White Rose Lane the footpath from Maybury used to cross open fields to the plank bridge over the Hoe Bourne. Now the houses and gardens of White Rose Lane run along either side of the footpath. The school playing fields occupy the land beyond the stream, where the common fields of Woking were once farmed.

Pathfields to Old Woking.

131.   This photograph, taken in the summer of 1899, shows a group of farmers cutting hay in the fields
where Rydens Way is today. The line of trees in the background marks the end of Rydens Way, where James
Walker's Hoe Bridge works are now.

132.   This picture of the Monument, on Monument Hill, is probably the oldest published photograph of Woking. It dates from the 1860s, before the 60 ft.-tower disappeared. This was built by Sir Edward Zouch during the reign of James I, but its function is uncertain. It may have been a beacon light to guide messengers from Oatlands Palace to Hoe Place, where the king often stayed, or perhaps it was a prospect tower. Its precise location has never been proved. Excavation in 1960 to try to discover its remains failed and old maps of the area show it in various places. Even its final days are uncertain. Some books state that it was taken down in 1867, others that it fell down in a storm in 1867 or 1868.

133.   The staff of Poundfield House. In the centre of the picture is Edward Ryde, the owner of Poundfield House from 1865 until his death in 1892. Edward Ryde was born in Woking in 1822. He trained as a surveyor and eventually became involved in work on several railways, notably the South Eastern Railway. He served as a churchwarden, was on the local school board and in 1892 was elected onto Surrey County Council. His diaries, dating from 1844-92, are on loan to the Surrey Records Office at Guildford and provide a fascinating insight into the life of Woking in the late 19th century.

# SATURDAY, AUG. 8th, 1925

# GARDEN FÊTE

## POUNDFIELD, WOKING VILLAGE,

### in the Garden of St. George's Home and the adjoining Field

(by kind permission of the Home Committee and the Woking Urban District Council).

## IN THE FIELD.

*CHILDREN'S SPORTS* (3 p.m.)

Events include :—

Flat Races, Boys aged 5–7, 7–10, 10–14

    "     Girls aged   "    "    "

High Jump, Boys

    "     Girls

Egg and Spoon Race, Girls

Kangaroo Race, Boys

Sack Race, Boys

Flower Pot Race, Boys and Girls

Costume Race, Mixed

*ADULTS' SPORTS* (*evening*).

Ladies' Egg and Spoon

Haricot Race, Gent.'s

Blind Driving, Mixed, etc., etc.

*Entries taken on the Field.*  *Prizes according to Entries.*

Entrance Fees for all races 3d., with the exception of the 5–7, 7–10 Flat Races, when it will be 1d. and 2d. respectively.

Draw for Large Doll's House at 4.30 p.m.     Cocoanut Shies.     Hoop La.
Crazy Kitchen.    Aunt Sally.    Competitions.    Lemonade.

## TEAS, 4 to 6 p.m., 6d. each person.

## IN THE GARDEN.

### The BAND OF MAYFORD SCHOOL will be in attendance

(Under the direction of Mr. E. A. Brown).

#### Handicraft Exhibition.    Fortune Teller.    Stalls:

Fancy Goods, Fairy Well, Sweets, Ices, Lemonade, Hat Trimming Competition.

## DANCING ON THE LAWN 7 TILL 9 P.M.

### Entire Proceeds to the WOKING DISTRICT NURSE CLUB.

● ●   *In the event of wet weather, there will be accommodation under cover.*   ● ●

## SOMETHING GOING ON ALL THE TIME.

Slocombe Bros., Printers, 97, Vale Farm Road, Woking.

134. Notice for a garden fete at Poundfield House, printed in 1925.

135. Church Street showing the village school, built in 1848, and, in the background, the parish church of St Peter. The first record of Woking appears in A.D. 708-715 when there was a monastery somewhere in the area. Its location is still unknown but a number of places have been suggested, including St Peter's church. The church is perhaps the most likely site as it is known that the monastery was also dedicated to St Peter.

136. The High Street, looking from the junction with Church Street. Sir James Zouch obtained a market charter for the town of Woking (now Old Woking) and built the Market House opposite the entrance to Church Street. In about 1908 it was replaced by the cottages seen on the right of this picture. Although no trace of the 17th-century building can be found in their roof timbers, there is evidence to suggest that part of the walls of the Market House still survives in the recently-restored cottages.

137. (*above*) The High Street, looking from the corner of Broadmead Road into the village centre. The small cottage on the right was demolished in about 1948. The building opposite was the *Hand and Spear* public house and was owned by Mr. J. Gunning from 1908 to 1916. The local scout troop, formed in 1914, at one time had its headquarters in this building before moving to its present hut in 1922.

138. (*right*) The High Street at the junction with Broadmead Road where the mini-roundabout is today. The building on the left, Conway West Motors, was at one time part of the *White Horse Hotel*, a 17th-century inn. Mr. Conway West purchased the hotel from the brewery, Lascelles, Tickner & Co. Ltd., in 1923 and converted it into his garage.

139. (*above*) A. C. Fleming's garage, High Street. In 1931 Conway West sold the garage to Mr. A. C. T. Fleming, who stayed here until 1939 when the Woking Urban District Council purchased the site for road improvements. Part of the building can still be seen in Leigh's Service Garage.

140. (*below*) The High Street, looking towards the junction with Broadmead Road, with the Old Manor House on the left. The Old Manor House dates from the 17th century with 18th-century additions to the right. It should not be confused with the Manor of Woking at Woking Palace, or with Hoe Place, where the lords of the manor lived. One writer suggests that the house shown here was probably the 'steward of the manor's house'.

141. In the late 19th and early 20th centuries many villages and works had their own brass bands; Unwin Brothers were no exception. This photograph shows the Gresham Press band which won a marching and playing competition at Aldershot in 1906. They also became the southern area champions. Unfortunately, the band was not re-formed after the First World War.

The Floods, Woking Village

142. (*above*) The floods in the High Street. In the early part of this century this part of the village often flooded. Many old photographs survive, notably of the winter of 1928 and, in more recent times, 1968. In the past, horses and carts were used to ferry people along the road to dry land near the village centre or towards Kingfield.

143. (*below*) Old Woking High Street, looking from the *Crown and Anchor* towards Kingfield. The Old Woking Service Station would now be on the corner to the right. Nearly all the houses on the left still remain, only a few new ones have been built, but the quiet village street has been lost forever with the introduction of motor vehicles.

144.  Vicarage Lane, looking towards the junction with Kingfield Road and Old Woking High Street. This photograph was taken on 26 October 1928 for Woking Urban District Council and is one of a large collection of old photographs owned by the council showing Woking in the 1920s and 1930s. Many of the pictures show roads before and after they were repaired or developed.

145.  The Kingfield Stores on the corner of Stockers Lane and Kingfield Road. This photograph, taken during the First World War, is a reminder of the days when every village had its own village stores or corner shop. The old enamel signs, advertising Lascelles, Tickner & Co., mineral waters, Fry's chocolate and cocoa, and R. White's lemonade, have sadly gone and the shop has now become a fancy-dress and costume centre.

146. A class of children at Westfield School in 1920. The first school in Westfield was opened in 1849 as a National School, and has now been converted into a chapel. The present school on the opposite side of Westfield Road was built in 1897. The site was bought by the Woking School Board from Gustav Wermig, Woking Council's first chairman, for £350. The school was built with bricks from the brickfields in Jackman's Nursery at Goldsworth.

147.   Bonner's Farm and outbuildings, with the common land in the foreground. Westfield got its name from one of the common fields of Woking. The lower west field covered the area of Westfield Avenue, whilst upper west field occupied the land where the schools are now. King field and the town field, to the north of Kingfield Road and the High Street, were the town's other two common fields.

Sutton Place, The Gallery

148.   The manor of Sutton, first mentioned in the Domesday Book of 1086, was from the late 13th century onwards held with the manor of Woking. In 1329 the Manor House at Sutton was described as ruinous and, when it was finally separated from Woking in 1520, a new house had to be built. This house, called Sutton Place, was built by Sir Richard Weston. It originally surrounded a square courtyard but the north gateway was destroyed by fire and pulled down in the 1780s. The buildings that remain are now owned by Mr. Stanley Seeger and run by the Sutton Place Heritage Trust.

Fox & Hounds, Sutton.

149.   The *Fox and Hounds* at Sutton Green looks from the outside more or less the same today, but inside modern furnishings and recent redecoration makes it popular with more than just the local labourers and estate workers who frequented it in the past. The present public house was built in 1904.

KEMISHFORD

150.   The old cottages and houses at Kemishford have remained largely unaltered since this photograph was taken in the early years of this century. The old bridge nearby, built in 1858, still carries traffic over the Stanford Brook, beside the original Kemishford.

151. Prey Heath Road, with the railway arch in the distance. In 1838 plans were made for a branch railway line from Woking to Guildford. It was to be completely level and would have needed an embankment 42 ft. high to cross the Stanford Brook at Mayford. Fortunately the scheme was dropped and in 1843 a new plan was put forward and a line built in 1845 by the London & South Western Railway. The drive to Worplesdon station is on the right of the picture, just before the arch. The station was opened in 1883.

152.   The *Mayford Arms*, looking from the junction of Guildford Road and Westfield Road. The old Mayford Bridge is just visible in the distance. It was replaced in 1926-7 by the present structure but the foundations of the old brick arch can still be seen in the bed of the stream. The *Mayford Arms* was built in 1905 when the original inn was turned into a private house.

153. Many villages in this area had their own ponds on the village green or beside the road. This one in Mayford was outside Havelock Cottages, Egley Road, opposite the entrance to Jackman's Garden Centre.

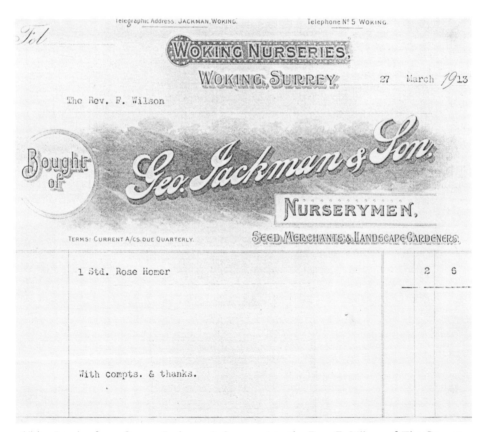

154. Invoice from George Jackman & Son, sent to the Rev. F. Wilson of The Grange, Old Woking, in 1913.

WATER SPLASH
HOOK HEATH

155.   The watersplash near the junction of Hook Heath Road and Saunders Lane. Although the small stream
has now been piped under the road, the memory of the old ford still remains in the name on a pillar box nearby.
It was the last ford in Woking to disappear, others, such as at Mayford, Pyrford, and Durnford, in Horsell, being
replaced by bridges long before.

Hook Heath Farm, Woking.

F.Blumfields.
Photo Series 655.

156. (*above*) Hook Heath Farm, looking from Woking Golf Club along Pond Road with 'Jesse's Pond' on the right. Hook Heath Farm is now a convalescent and retirement home called 'Tamerton'.

157. (*below*) The high class area of the borough is also the highest part of the borough geographically. Hook Heath was in the 17th and 18th centuries a squatter settlement, with tinkers, gipsies and many poor, untidy cottages. In the 1880s, however, when the London Necropolis & National Mausoleum Company sold the land, it was marketed as ideal for large, expensive houses. It was a secluded area, with good views to the south towards the Downs and in 1893 it also boasted its own golf club. From the late 1890s to the First World War, Hook Heath grew rapidly, with many large Victorian and Edwardian houses being built.

Hook Heath, Woking.     6.A.

YORK ROAD, WOKING.

158. (*above*) York Road, looking from
Wych Hill towards the town. The York
Estate was laid out in 1893, the year the
Duke and Duchess of York (later King
George V and Queen Mary) were married.
It was described in the sale catalogue as
'adjoining the favoured Mount Hermon
area' but, whilst Mount Hermon Road
ran along its southern boundary, the rail-
way marked its northern edge, making
York Road less attractive than the other
roads in the area.

159. (*right*) Wych Hill, in the days when
there were few motor cars on Woking's
roads. As the traffic increased and the
roads were repaired and widened, the
quiet country lanes began to disappear.
A few still survive and, like the old photographs in this book, they should be preserved for ever.

160. (*above*) Turnoak Corner, where the Turnoak roundabout is today. The round-
about was the first to be built in Woking. It was approved in 1930 by the Woking
Urban District Council and completed in the autumn of 1934. This photograph was
taken in the early years of this century and shows the road to Old Woking, winding its
way past Victorian houses on the left and open fields on the right. Guildford Road to
Woking station is on the left and Egley Road to Mayford and Guildford goes to the
right.

161. (*below*) Guildford Hill, looking from near the *Cotteridge Hotel* down the hill
towards where N.E.U. Engineering are today. This picture was taken in the days when
the only traffic on Woking's busiest road consisted of a donkey cart, a pony and trap,
and a horse and haycart.

Guildford Road, Woking

162.  The peace celebrations of 1919 must have been a marvellous sight. Photographs of the event have survived showing the decorations in Chertsey Road and Commercial Road and the games in Woking Park. This picture shows an archway built across Guildford Road by the junction with Hill View Road. The *Cotteridge Hotel*, on the corner with Constitution Hill, can be seen in the background.

163.  The *Railway Hotel* was built in 1840 by Edward Woods. It was the first building to be erected on Woking Common after the opening of Woking station. The old hotel has since been rebuilt and is now called the *Sovereign*.

# DEVELOPING

*You can get the Camera you want at Harper's*

The NEW Kodak

## Six-20 Junior

(in two models)

With Doublet Lens **37/6**

With f 6·3 Anastigmat Lens **55/-**

The "Beau" Brownie

The Box Camera with the better lens. **21/-**
In Black, Blue or Brown.

# PRINTING

*You can get the Camera you want at Harper's*

**ENSIGN SELFIX CAMERA**

The newest Ensign
(In three models)

Anastigmat Lenses

f. 7·7 lens **40/-**
f. 6·3 lens **52/6**
f. 4·5 lens **70/-**

## Zeiss-Ikon Cameras

16 Pictures on 8 exposure films

**BABY BOX TENGOR**
takes 16 pictures on V.P.K. Film **18/6**

**BOX TENGOR**
takes 16 pictures on 2 Brownie Film **22/6**

**BABY IKONTA**
takes 16 pictures on V.P.K. Film from **£3 : 7 : 6**

**IKONTA**
takes 16 pictures on 2 Brownie Film from **£4:10:0**

**ENSIGN REFLEX CAMERA**

with f. 4·5 lens.

Focal plane shutter speeded to 1/500 sec.

**£6 : 17 : 6**

# ENLARGING

# GEORGE HARPER, *The Kodak Dealer*
## 29, GUILDFORD ROAD, WOKING

164.   George Harper advertisement taken from a local newspaper published in 1933.

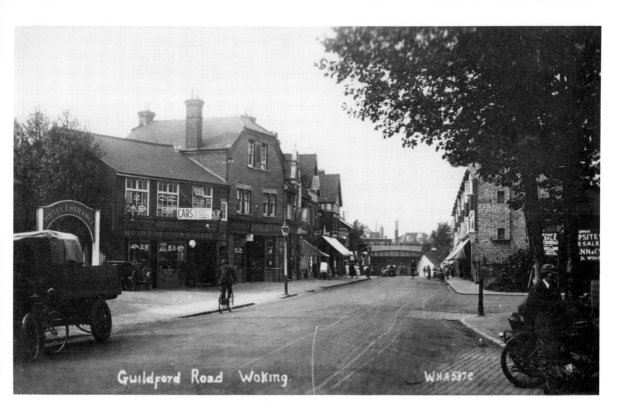

165. (*above*) Guildford Road, looking towards Victoria Arch from outside the *Railway Hotel*. Boorman & Sons' Mount Hermon Garage is on the left along with the shops now replaced by Merion House. The shops opposite still remain. The plot of land on the right was later built on, as the next picture shows.

166. (*below*) In this picture the land on the corner of Guildford Road and Station Approach houses Conway West Motors. Conway West began in Old Woking in 1912 with just one employee, but business grew after the First World War and in 1928 this garage was built. By 1934 the firm employed over 50 people. Part of Boorman's and the *Railway Hotel* can be seen on the left of this picture.

167. Guildford Road, Station Approach and the Technical School from the air. Guildford Road and Victoria Arch can be seen on the left with the land where Lynton House is now behind the shops of Guildford Road. Station Approach crosses the picture from the bottom left to the top right, where the station can just be seen. Maxwell's shop is on the corner of Station Approach and Heathside Road. Maxwell's started trading in Woking in 1896 and moved to this site in 1906. The Technical School, or Boys' Grammar School, was opened on 15 July 1914 with places for 300 boys. The school finally closed in 1977.

168. The original St Dunstan's church was an iron chapel opened in January 1899 in Percy Street. It was built by the Rev. W. D. Allanson, who also paid for the presbytery in Church Street. When Father Plummer came to Woking in 1923 he found the old presbytery riddled with damp and decided to purchase Lavender Cottage in Heathside Crescent. He then sold the Church Street premises to Woking Urban District Council which used it in 1928 for its new fire station. On 11 November 1924 Father Plummer cut the first sod for the foundation of a new church in White Rose Lane, next to Lavender Cottage. Five months later, on 26 April 1925, the new Roman Catholic church was opened. This photograph was taken in the summer of 1926.

THEATRE TICKET OFFICE.
TELEPHONE: 114 WOKING.

Jan. '12

# To MAXWELL & SONS,

## Pianoforte, Organ and Music Sellers,

### MENDELSSOHN HOUSE, WOKING.

And at WIMBLEDON.

Sole Agents for—
THE CECILIAN,
The Perfect Piano Player.

Sole Agents for—
THE AUTOPIANO.

Sole Agents for—
THE GRAMOPHONE Co
"His Master's Voice."

PIANOS by BROADWOOD, BRINSMEAD, COLLARD, BECHSTEIN, BLUTHNER, STEINWAY, SCHIEDMAYER, KNAUSS, LIPP, and other eminent makers, at the Lowest Prices for Cash, or on the Hire System.

| | | | | | |
|---|---|---|---|---|---|
| Dec. 12 | 4 Scout Bugles, with cords. | | 1 | 16 | 0 |

PIANOS
For Sale or Hire, or on the
Hire Purchase System.
*Pianos for Concerts and
Entertainments.*

✦ ✦ ✦

TUNING:
Pianos Tuned by the Year,
*One Guinea,*
Or Single Tunings.

Harmoniums & American
Organs Tuned & Repaired.

✦ ✦ ✦

MUSIC:
All the best
New and Standard Works
kept in Stock.

✦ ✦ ✦

PIANO REPAIRS:
Estimates Free.

✦ ✦ ✦

PIANOS EXCHANGED.

✦ ✦ ✦

MUSICIANS
PROVIDED.

RECEIVED WITH THANKS

MAR 22 1912

MAXWELL & SONS.

169.   Invoice from Maxwell & Sons sent to Major Hamilton for the Mayford scout troop in 1912.

170. (*above*) The rebuilding of Woking's railway station by Trollope & Colls of Dorking in 1936-7. Woking station had to be rebuilt as the railway line was being electrified. The first electric service through Woking took place on 4 July 1937. The new fast and frequent train service was a major factor in Woking's development.

171. (*below*) Although this photograph was taken at Bolton, Lancashire, it does nevertheless illustrate an important part of Woking's sporting past. On 11 January 1908 Woking F.C. met Bolton Wanderers in the F.A. Cup. Unfortunately Woking lost the match, but this historic picture has at least been saved for posterity—as have all the pictures in this collection of the Woking of bygone days.